Expecting God's Surprises

Expecting God's
Surprises

Devotions for the Advent Journey

Robert E. Dunham

11/09

G
GENEVA

Geneva Press
Louisville, Kentucky

Book design by Sharon Adams
Cover design by PAZ Design Group

First edition
Published by Geneva Press
Louisville, Kentucky

This book is printed on acid-free paper that meets the American National Standards Institute Z39.48 standard. ∞

PRINTED IN THE UNITED STATES OF AMERICA

02 03 04 05 06 07 08 09 10 — 10 9 8 7 6 5 4 3 2

Library of Congress Cataloging-in-Publication Data

Dunham, Robert E., 1948–
    Expecting God's surprises : devotions for the Advent journey/ Robert E. Dunham.—1st ed.
       p.   cm.
    Includes bibliographical references.
    ISBN 0-664-50177-X (alk. paper)
    1. Advent—Prayer-books and devotions—English. I. Title.
BV40.D86 2001
242'.332—dc21
                                                        2001023129

Contents

Introduction

Despite the concerted efforts of liturgical scholars, preachers, and church musicians, the season of Advent has still not gained much of a foothold in many American churches. The most obvious reason for such failure is that Advent's celebration is a profoundly countercultural act. While the churches are trying to articulate an emphasis on watching, waiting, and preparation during the weeks after Thanksgiving, the shopping malls have been piping in Christmas music ever since Halloween. Newspapers have been counting down the shopping days. L. L. Bean, J. Crew, and Land's End have already mailed three or four holiday catalogs each. The Christmas train has been barreling down the tracks for quite some time, and it's not going to stop until Christmas Day or, more likely, until the post-Christmas sales are over.

So how in the world can the Christian church expect to have any success in slowing down the grand procession long enough to address the themes of Advent? In all truthfulness, it cannot. Many worship planners threw in the towel years ago and started singing Christmas carols the Sunday after Thanksgiving. Is that so bad? Well, no and yes. No, because we all know Christmas is coming, and it *is* one of the two most important festivals in the Christian year, and it deserves a proper celebration. On the other hand, when we rush right into Christmas without a proper consideration of the themes of Advent, we miss some texts and tunes that help us to focus on one of the most important, though sometimes perplexing, facets of the Christian faith. I am speaking of eschatology, the consideration of the consummation of history, of final destinies and last things. Advent, you see, not only looks backward to the coming of Christ at Bethlehem, but forward to his second coming at the end of time. Advent is not just a period of Christmas preliminaries, but a season in its own right. It is a season of waiting in a culture that does not like to wait, and thus waits poorly if at all. It is a season of thoughtful preparation in a culture that pushes more and more emphatically for action and bottom lines. Jon Walton, a friend and pastoral colleague, once called Advent "a quirky season slightly out of step with the world."

> Its colors are not red and green, but purple, moody and dark. Its music is minor chord, not major. And its theme is repentance and preparation, not "deck the halls." . . . It is a season . . . focused on the coming of Jesus, on

his arrival not only in Bethlehem two thousand years ago, but also his coming again, and his arrival in our lives today.[1]

If that is the mood and spirit of Advent, then how shall we celebrate rightly? If preparation is the name of the game, what shall we do to prepare? If expectation is the watchword of Advent, what do we expect? Whom do we expect? And how does what happened in preparation for the first Christmas inform and shape our preparation in this time of year? The answers to such questions are not as apparent as we might think. In fact, Advent watchfulness and preparation are demanding and difficult tasks, in part because we have deeply embedded preconceptions of the One for whom we are waiting and watching.

Barbara Brown Taylor illustrates something of the problem with a true story of a game devised by scientists.

Here is how it goes. They sit you down at a table in front of an ordinary deck of cards and they flash six of them at you, asking you to identify them as fast as you can—nine of diamonds, three of hearts, jack of clubs—whoops! What was that one? Then they repeat the exercise, slowing it down a little so you can get the ones you missed the first time.

The third time is so slow that you think you must be an idiot because there is one card you simply cannot identify. You think you know what it is, but you are not sure, and it is not until the cards are laid on the table in front of you that you can see what the problem is. The mystery card is a six of spades, only it is red, not black. The deck has been fixed. Someone has changed the rules, rules that prevented you from seeing what was there. You could not see a red spade because spades are supposed to be black.

Our expectations, however faithful, may prevent us from seeing what is there.[2]

We come to Advent with any number of precon-ceptions about the season, about the One whom it heralds, about ourselves. The trick is to allow those ideas to inform but not hinder our ability to discern the new thing God may be doing in our midst. The first lesson of Advent is openness to God's surprise.

The daily devotional meditations that follow are governed by that larger theme of surprise in the midst of our expectations. I hope the reader will find the daily reflections helpful in his or her own journey through Advent. I offered them first as a gift of gratitude to the congregation of University Presbyterian Church in Chapel Hill, North Carolina, for the remarkable privilege of serving as a pastor and friend in their midst through most of the 1990s. I prepared many of the devotional meditations during a summer sabbatical, another gift and privilege for which I continue to be deeply grateful. I am indebted to my family for putting up with me during my summer of reading and writing, and particularly to my daughter Leah, whose honest critique and able proofreading have helped shape and improve this booklet. And I am thankful for the friends and colleagues whose insights, words, and stories grace these pages. As the reader will discern from the notes, many of those friends are part of a remarkable group of preachers known as the Moveable Feast, a lectionary study group of men and women from all across America with whom I have had the privilege of working for more than a dozen years now. My relationship with those colleagues has been as important to me as life's blood over the course of time. They have taught me how to live before God's word, waiting for discernment, learning the discipline of study and prayer, and cultivating an expectation of God's surprise.

I have brought that same expectation to the preparation of this devotional book. My hope is that others who read what follows will find God stirring them in a particular way this Advent. Advent awaits us. I invite the reader to join me as we undertake a journey together—with eyes and ears and hearts wide open to the mystery of God's grace.

DAY ONE *(First Sunday of Advent)*
Reading: Matthew 24:36–44

I spent my childhood, like many children, anxious for Christmas to hurry up and get here. But I did so with at least some fear and trembling. I think what caused the anxiety for me were the annual refrains of the old children's song, "Santa Claus Is Comin' to Town." You know the song: "Oh, you better watch out, / you better not cry, / you better not pout, / I'm telling you why: / Santa Claus is comin' to town!" There was promise in that song, but there was also warning: "He sees you when you're sleepin', / he knows when you're awake, / He knows if you've been bad or good, / so be good for goodness sake." The message of the song, obviously written by a parent skilled in the art of motivation by fear, was very clear to me: Get excited! But shape up!

Clearly something of the same dynamic is at work in the season of Advent. It is a season of wonderful promise, augmented with a healthy dose of warning, about One who is coming. It is a time of joy and anticipation, but it is also a season of repentance and self-examination. On the

First Sunday of Advent each year, the church's lectionary always draws us to texts that lean hard upon the warnings, texts that speak of the return of Christ and the final consummation of human history. This reading from Matthew's Gospel is a case in point, our annual warning shot across the bow to remind us to be alert, to watch, to prepare ourselves. "You must be ready," Jesus says, "for the Son of Man is coming at an unexpected hour." In other words, "You better watch out."

Matthew's accent is on the unexpected time and circumstance of Christ's return, and clearly his concern is that the church be prepared. The images Jesus uses (a flood, a thief) are pointed, intrusive, disturbing images with which to begin the season, but they are helpful in calling us to be alert, to make preparation for "uncertain certainties."[3] There is the sound of judgment here but also the promise of good news. Matthew's community had been waiting for the day of Christ's return, and their repeated question was "When?" The answer Matthew remembered for them from Christ's teaching was, "about that day and hour no one knows" (v. 36). The more important issue, he argued, was how they would live in the delay, and his clear call to them was to live as those who were prepared for that day, ready to give account for their lives.

Though the centuries have now intervened, the message is essentially the same for us. Jon Walton says of this passage:

> The Son of Man is coming at an unexpected hour. And it's not that you shouldn't take out a thirty-year mortgage, or sign for the five-year payment plan on the new car. It's not that you shouldn't subscribe to the new season at the symphony or not expect to see all twelve deliveries in the fruit-of-the-month club from Harry and David's. The point is not to stake your life on it. Stake your life on the faith that the end of things belongs to God who is coming to us at almost any time if we can only have the wits to pay attention, and that at some point not yet in sight we shall give account to that God of all that we are.[4]

Prayer

O God, the days grow shorter and the night comes more quickly in these days. Teach us what it means to watch and wait for Your coming in our lives. Amen.

DAY TWO

Reading: Matthew 25:31–46

The German pastor Dietrich Bonhoeffer spent his final days imprisoned in a Nazi concentration camp because of his open opposition to doctrines and practices of the Third Reich. In a 1943 letter posthumously published as one of his *Letters and Papers from Prison*, Bonhoeffer described his prison experience in terms evocative of this season. From his prison cell, he wrote, "One waits and hopes and putters around. But in the end what we do is of little consequence. The door is shut, and it can be opened only from the outside."[5]

Bonhoeffer's point, of course, was that humankind's final destiny is ultimately in God's hands, not ours. In that fact is great comfort, the comfort of Advent: that ultimately the kingdom is God's to give and not ours to build. On that grand cosmic stage our part may seem trivial, but I would take issue with Bonhoeffer as to its significance and consequence. In counterpoint, our reading today presents Christ's vision of the importance of our small, unremembered acts along the way.

Ultimately, God's kingdom will come on earth.

Ultimately, Christ will return to establish the reign of peace and wholeness. That is the affirmation of our faith. But in the meantime, we are called to live as though that day were here. One of my mentors, Presbyterian theologian Albert Curry Winn, said once of such hope and anticipation:

> Since this is the way it is going to be ultimately and finally, let us begin now. If we are to be judged by how we have treated the least of these, Christ's brothers and sisters, let us begin now to reevaluate who's important. Let us approximate justice. Let us practice compassion. Let us stop worrying so much about what people will think and what people may say and what the newspaper may publish. Let us ask what the Judge will think and what the Judge will say.[6]

New York City's Abyssinian Baptist Church is a strong and creative African American congregation that gathers for worship on 125th Street in Harlem. The church building is a great monument to hope in a neighborhood that has experienced significant decay, but, more important, the leaders and members of the church have taken Christ's challenge seriously in some substantial ways. They have organized a locally owned bank, since none of the commercial banks will locate in the neighborhood. They have set up after-school and summer programs for latchkey kids in neighborhood high-rise apartments. They have put together neighborhood redevelopment agencies and started Bible studies in housing projects. In short, they have attended to both the physical and spiritual needs of the people who form their community.

A reporter from the *New York Times* tracked down the church's pastor, Calvin Butts, one day. In a question that echoed Bonhoeffer's comments about "puttering around" with "little consequence," the reporter said to Butts, "Look, you're doing great things, but it's hard to see what difference it's making; so what enables you and your folks to keep going?" Calvin Butts said, "Here's what. We've read the Bible and we know how it ends. We aren't at the end yet, but we know how it ends, and that's what makes the difference."[7]

What do we expect? And how does it govern how we will live between the hope and the fulfillment?

Prayer
Filled with the promise of Advent, help us to live now as those who trust Your promise and who seek to be faithful to the life to which You call us. Amen.

DAY THREE
Reading: Mark 8:27–30

After the disciples had summarized the public opinion about Jesus, he asked them, "But who do you say that I am?" Of all the questions asked in scripture, this one pursues me relentlessly. And though this reading from Mark's Gospel is not a classic Advent text, it does lay bare our assumptions in this season of expectations. Who do we say that Jesus is? What do we expect of him? What are we willing to do for him in gratitude for what he has done for us? How will we live as his disciples?

Yesterday's reflection on our role in God's cosmic plan offered us another question that seems germane to our reading today. If God is shaping the future, what difference does it make who we say Jesus is? What can we contribute to that future? Today I offer two well-worn stories that help shape a possible answer.

The first is drawn from an Advent sermon preached by Archbishop Desmond Tutu of South Africa:

> Often in an orchestra there are all kinds of instruments—oboes, cellos, violins and the

like. The members of the orchestra are usually dolled up in formal wear, and sometimes in the back of the orchestra is someone equally formally togged out carrying a triangle. The orchestra will sound off and the conductor will be creating all those wonderful sounds . . . and now and again the conductor will point to our friend in the back who will strike the triangle—ping. Now that may seem to be an insignificant contribution, but in the conception of the artist something quite unique and indispensable would be missing if that ping did not sound when it should. And so we say to our people back home, black and white, "only you can love God as you can. Not even your identical twin can stand in for you. And something quite indispensable would be missing from heaven if your kind of loving of God were missing."[8]

The other story was told by Robert Fulghum, that wonderful storyteller, in his book, *It Was on Fire When I Lay Down on It.* It has to do with an Italian traveler who came to the French town of Chartres during the days when the town's great cathedral was being constructed.

Arriving at the end of the day he went to the site just as the workmen were leaving for home. He asked one man, covered with dust, what he did there. The man replied that he was a stonemason. He spent his days carving rocks. Another man, when asked, said he was a glassblower who spent his days making slabs of colored glass. Still another workman replied that he was a blacksmith who pounded iron for a living.

Wandering into the deepening gloom of the unfinished edifice, the traveler came upon an older woman, armed with a broom, sweeping up the stone chips and wood shavings and glass shards from the day's work. "What are you doing?" he asked.

The woman paused, leaning on her broom, and looking up toward the high arches, replied, "Me? I'm building a cathedral for the Glory of Almighty God."[9]

"Who do you say that I am?" Jesus asked. In Advent our answer reveals not only our hope but also something of who *we* are, of what we expect, and of what we are willing to do as we live toward that expectation.

Prayer

We come, O God, to play our part in the great drama of redemption, however large, however small. Guide us, lead us, we pray. Amen.

DAY FOUR
Reading: Psalm 122

I don't know how many people keep Advent wreaths in their homes these days. For a long time now at our house we have made a practice of lighting the candles of the wreath at every gathered evening meal—the first candle throughout the first week of Advent, the first and second candles during the second, and so on. This week in worship and in some of our homes we have lit the first candle of the Advent wreath—the candle of hope. In this week we look back at Bethlehem and forward to Christ's return, and we do so in hope.

Hope is such a powerful force in the lives of individuals and communities, for it keeps them looking forward. There is nothing so moving and reassuring as a community forged by a common hope, and there is nothing quite so bleak as a person or community in which hope has been lost.

The psalmist in today's reading describes hope in terms of entering Jerusalem and living within God's reign of *shalom* ("peace"). For the psalmist, to enter Jerusalem is to enter a new world of joy and peace, despite all the old realities of hatred and war all around. It is to live full of hope in God's future, despite any evidence that suggests that one should do otherwise. Old Testament scholar Clint McCann finds a powerful illustration of what it means to enter into this kind of Jerusalem, to live hopefully toward God's future, in Walker Percy's novel, *The Second Coming.* He discerns such movement in the character of Will Barrett, whose father committed suicide when Will was young and who has struggled for a long time with a voice inside him that keeps telling him to do the same. "The voice knows what the world is like":

> Come, what else is there [except suicide]? What other end if you don't make the end? Make your own bright end in this dying world, this foul and feckless place, where you know as well as I that nothing ever really works, that you were never once yourself and never will be. . . . Come, close it out before it closes you out, because believe me life does no better job with dying than with living. Close it out. At least you can do that, not only lose but win, with one last splendid gesture defeat the whole foul feckless world.

Will responds to the voice with a simple No. It is

a No based on the experience of a genuine love between himself and another, which he takes as a sign that "the Lord is here."[10] Over against the allure of hopelessness, Will takes his stand with hope. Confident not only of God's presence but also of God's purpose in its history and its future, the Christian church takes its Advent stand today. Because we hope, we live.

Christian hope is not naïve. It shares, understands, and partakes in the world's sufferings, pains, and defeats, but perseveres on account of a great "nevertheless." It combines what biblical scholar Walter Brueggemann refers to as "utter realism and extravagant hope."[11] More than a decade ago, well before the revolution that led to his becoming the Czech president, Vaclav Havel wrote:

> Hope is . . . not the same as joy that things are going well, or a willingness to invest in enterprises that are obviously headed for early success, but, rather, an ability to work for something because it is good, not just because it stands a chance to succeed. The more unpropitious the situation in which we demonstrate hope, the deeper that hope is. Hope is definitely not the same thing as opti-

mism. It is not the conviction that something will turn out well, but the certainty that something makes sense, regardless of how it turns out. In short, I think that the deepest and most important form of hope, the only one that can keep us above water and urge us to good works, and the only true source of the breathtaking dimension of the human spirit and its efforts, is something we get, as it were, from "elsewhere." It is . . . this hope, above all, which gives us strength to live and continually try new things, even in conditions that seem as hopeless as ours do.[12]

Such is the hope of Advent, the hope that propels us onward in our journey, but our "elsewhere" has a particular name, Jesus, and a particular human face, seen first at Bethlehem.

Prayer

You are the source of our hope, O God, and Yours is the future toward which we journey. Fill us with hope, we pray, and make steady our steps. Amen.

DAY FIVE

Reading: Isaiah 40:1–5

These wonderful words of comfort and promise have provided sustenance and encouragement for God's people in all kinds of circumstances. They have helped people find their way through exiles both imposed by others and self-imposed. And their promise—that the ups and downs will be leveled, that the crooked ways will be made straight, and that God's glory will be revealed—has helped people look beyond whatever torments, trials, and tribulations they were experiencing in their current terrain. Isaiah's prophecy has provided and still provides welcome words in all circumstances of distress.

In the age of enlightenment, however, these words have also been dismissed as wishful thinking, as a fantasy and nothing more. Thus, if we are to claim Isaiah's old vision and its fulfillment in Jesus Christ, we will need to be prepared to stand counterculturally with our hopes.

Fellow preacher Lee Wyatt pointed me several years ago to one of C. S. Lewis's Narnia children's stories for an example of how one takes such a stand, shaped by a story. In *The Silver Chair*, the great lion Aslan, Lewis's narrative Christ-figure, sends Jill Pole and Eustace Scrubb to Narnia on a mission to rescue Prince Rilian, who has been charmed into servitude to the Queen of the Underworld. They are sent to help the prince return to his true vocation as King of the Overland.

On their journey, Jill and Eustace acquire several companions from Narnia, most notably Puddleglum, a Marsh-wiggle. If you know Lewis's stories, you know that despite their strange names, the characters bear keen resemblance to the folks you and I encounter every day. In any event, the rescue team finally reaches Prince Rilian, frees him, and then attempts to escape—only to be intercepted by the Queen. With all her charm and enchanting spells, she tries to persuade the rescue party that the Underworld really is all there is, that there is no Overland, except in their dreams. There is no sun, she insists, no Aslan, no Narnia. The party is about to give in, so convincing is she, until Puddleglum acts decisively. He stamps out the fire on which the Queen has cast her enchanting powder, a brave and painful act, since Marsh-wiggles wear no shoes. And then he makes one of the most eloquent testimonies to hope, to a vision of truth, ever written. He speaks directly to the Queen:

> "One word, Ma'am," he said, coming back from the fire; limping, because of the pain. "One word. All you've been saying is quite right, I shouldn't wonder. I'm a chap who always liked to know the worst and then put the best face I can on it. So I won't deny any of what you said. But there's one thing more to be said, even so. Suppose we *have* only dreamed, or made up, all those things—trees and grass and sun and moon and stars and Aslan himself. Suppose we have. Then all I can say is that, in that case, the made-up things seem a good deal more important than the real ones. Suppose this black pit of a kingdom of yours *is* the only world. Well, it strikes me as a pretty poor one. And that's a funny thing, when you come to think of it. We're just babies making up a game, if you're right. But four babies playing a game can make a play world which licks your real world hollow. That's why I'm going to stand by the play world. I'm on Aslan's side even if there isn't any Aslan to lead it. I'm going to live as like a Narnian as I can even if there isn't any Narnia. So, thanking you kindly for our supper, if

these two gentlemen and the young lady are ready, we're leaving your court at once and setting out in the dark to spend our lives looking for Overland. Not that our lives will be very long, I should think; but that's small loss if the world's as dull a place as you say."[13]

What if we were to take our stand over against the cynicism and hopelessness of our time in behalf of Isaiah's vision? What if we, who have tasted something of God's reign, could be as bold as a Marsh-wiggle? I never thought I would ask the question exactly that way, but I believe old Puddleglum has a lesson to teach us. It is the church's steadfast conviction that Isaiah's vision will carry the day. Yet the question remains, Is it still the vision by which we want to shape our lives? Are we willing to live boldly into the future of God's design, setting out in the dark to spend our lives looking for Overland?

Prayer
O God, we believe. Help our unbelief. And help us to claim Your vision of life as it should be. Amen.

DAY SIX
Reading: Psalm 90

"So teach us to number our days that we may get a heart of wisdom" (RSV). The sobering words of the psalmist remind us that regardless of what we think and believe about the end of human history, *our own* human history has its limits; it has an end. Death comes apace to poets, plumbers, and presidents alike. Whether we like the assessment or not, novelist Clyde Edgerton's character Grove McCord has it right when he says, "You are history longer than you are fact."[14]

Though the focus of Advent is more cosmic, it has its personal dimensions too, and ultimately it leaves us with questions about our own destiny as we contemplate the future and end of all humankind. If Advent is to have a personal impact on me, I hope and trust that it will be a deeper sensitivity to the sacred in the seemingly mundane moments, and perhaps an ability to listen and look and notice more intentionally the good gifts of grace inherent in each and every day. That, I believe, is part of what the writer of the psalm means by a "heart of wisdom."

A while back I heard someone, long retired from a productive career, say, "A number of years ago I went off to college to get an education. I walked across the campus each day with great hurry so I could get to class. I went to class so I could make the grade. I made the grade to graduate. I graduated to get the job. I worked long and hard so I could retire. And here I am, wishing I could go back and walk that campus again." Surely most of us know what he meant. It was about the same time that a pastor-friend of mine observed that, in all his years of being a pastor, he had never heard anyone look back over their years and say, "I wish I had spent more time at the office."

History, *our* history, has an end. That fact need not fill us with dread or longing. One might hope that it would fill us with wonder, with gratitude, and with a determination to live each day with purpose and with a sense of awe. "So teach us to number our days that we may get a heart of wisdom."

Prayer
Confident of Your creative, sustaining grace, help us to live this day and every day with eyes wide open to Your goodness and with hearts wide open to Your love. Amen.

DAY SEVEN

Reading: Psalm 100

In 1560, William Kethe set out to write a hymn setting of Psalm 100, and the result was the still-familiar hymn, "All People That on Earth Do Dwell." Kethe's text eventually found its way to the lips of choristers and congregations when it was combined with a melody attributed to the composer Louis Bourgeois. (The tune, Old Hundredth, gained more permanence than the hymn and is sung almost weekly in many churches as the setting of an offertory Doxology.) Kethe did a good job of catching the feeling and flavor of the psalm in his text. I have to admit, however, that I never have been particularly crazy about the hymn's rather formal third verse:

> O enter then His gates with praise,
> Approach with joy His courts unto;
> Praise, laud, and bless His name always,
> For it is seemly so to do.

Though its meaning surely conveyed more power in the sixteenth century than it does today, "seemly" falls short, in my opinion, of capturing the spirit of gratitude at the heart of the psalmist's exhortation. But the hymn closes with a strong and memorable affirmation:

> For why? The Lord our God is good,
> His mercy is forever sure;
> His truth at all times firmly stood,
> And shall from age to age endure.[15]

It seems to me that in this Advent journey of grace and expectation, nothing will so prepare us to receive the news proclaimed in these days as a heart of gratitude. The season of Advent bids us survey past, present, and future for signs of God's goodness. It asks us to consider that God's truth and goodness have stood firmly throughout the most trying times in human history and "shall from age to age endure" to the very end of the human story.

We are entering into what many call "the season of giving." For us, to whom much has been given, grace upon grace, I might suggest that we consider this "a season of gratitude." The great Swiss theologian Karl Barth wrote:

> Grace and gratitude belong together like heaven and earth.

Grace evokes gratitude like the voice an echo.
Gratitude follows grace like thunder lightning.[16]

A season of gratitude in these days might just
make for a boisterous December storm beyond
our fondest memories or our best hopes.

Prayer
*Free us from all our frenetic quests, O God, and
help us to live this day with grace and gratitude.
Amen.*

DAY EIGHT *(Second Sunday of Advent)*
Reading: Matthew 3:1–12

There is a certain irony about the Second Sunday of Advent each year. As part of their morning liturgy, many churches light the second candle in the Advent wreath—the candle of peace. Then a few minutes later they read a Gospel text in which John the Baptist comes out of the wilderness to disturb the peace and call God's people then and God's people now to repentance. Every year about this time, into our desire for constancy and peace, John comes forward with fire in his eyes and change on his mind, saying, "The old is passing away; the new is pressing in upon us." Immediately we marshal the forces of resistance, for if there is one thing most of us avoid whenever we can, it is change.

We might like to get to Bethlehem without going first to the Jordan, but it is the only way there, and on this road one can't help but hear John's call for repentance and change.[17] I believe my pastor-friend Rick Spalding is right in his assessment that we resist John's message like the plague in these days and in his suggestion of what taking John's message to heart might mean for us:

This isn't a season that extends much of a welcome to proposals for change. (I found that out a few years ago when I tried to fiddle with the order of worship for Christmas Eve!) It wants to derive its comfort from the sameness and constancy of things, the silent peace of unmoving stars. The kind of change we're willing to contemplate is pocket change: easy to contain, easy to conceal. Pocket change is what we learn to practice in this season: practice *random* kindness, nothing systemic please! The sound that our pennies make as they clink against the bottom of the Salvation Army's red kettles is deafening.

But who told us that we could flee from the change to come? Stars *do* move. And the Presence we are presently preparing a way for *will change us*. That's what [John] is really trying to teach the crowds who come to him on Jordan's banks. . . .

"Prepare for major change" seems unlikely to replace "Merry Christmas" as the greeting of the season. But Jesus' birth made it impossible for people to think of God as an abstract intellectual exercise; and if we were to say so, to speak that truth aloud in this society at this time, *it would change us*.[18]

As we will see in the days and weeks ahead, one of the recurring emphases of the season of Advent is the call to repentance and change. And though we may run like the wind in the other direction at the thought, the change John has in mind may not so much disturb our peace as secure it.

Prayer

Break through our resistance, O God, and prepare our hearts for the new thing You are doing in our midst and within us. Amen.

DAY NINE

Reading: Luke 3:7–18

If change and repentance are the themes John the Baptist lends to our Advent journey, then surely one of the questions we may raise is, "What kind of repentance?" Biblical scholar and preacher Tom Long argues that the kind of repentance John preached

> is not a mid-course correction; it is more radical than that. The repentance John preached is not a repudiation of the past; it is more complex than that. The repentance John preached calls for a revision of the past. It calls us to look behind before we dare to move ahead. It calls for us to encounter the past we have lived through but not fully experienced, the past we have inherited but not inhabited, before we enter a future we do not yet comprehend.[19]

In other words, if we want to know what we should expect in Christ's return, it would be wise for us to turn back to the scriptures to understand more clearly and carefully the life of the One who came first at Bethlehem. To understand our own hearts in preparation for a second Advent, we need to look back at our own lives and try to discern there the signs of grace missed in the living of our days. Advent is an exercise not only of hope but also of memory. A good friend and colleague once noticed the meaning and benefit of such a revisitation:

> Whenever we are able to travel back across the landscape of our past, and to discover, in some memory, more evidence of the hand of God there than we first saw; more signs of grace there than we ever imagined being able to find; more incentive for living differently tomorrow in the light of this new encounter with some yesterday; then we have discovered repentance.[20]

Reexamining our past is seldom comfortable or easy, but without the repentance such hindsight invites, the future is a lot less promising than we may believe, and the good news of Bethlehem and Golgotha likely make a lot less sense. John knew that, and he offers his insight for all who have eyes to see and ears to hear.

Prayer
O God, our help in ages past, our hope for years to come, give us the vision we need to see Your hand in our past and Your light for the path before us. Amen.

DAY TEN
Reading: John 1:6–8

In one of his popular books, management guru Stephen Covey recounts an old story of the sea as told by a former seaman named Frank Koch. Koch tells of being on a battleship during training maneuvers. For several days the weather had been heavy and the visibility was poor with patchy fog. Koch remembers being on watch on the bridge one evening shortly before dark when a lookout on the other wing of the bridge spotted something. "Light, bearing on the starboard bow."

"Is it steady or moving astern?" the captain inquired. The lookout replied, "Steady, Captain." The meaning was clear; they were on a collision course. So the captain called to the signalman, "Signal that ship: We are on a collision course; advise you change course twenty degrees."

Back came the signal, "Advisable for you to change course twenty degrees." The captain said to the signalman, "Send, 'I am a captain; change course twenty degrees.'" "I'm a seaman second class," came the reply. "You had better change course twenty degrees."

By that time the captain was furious. He spat out, "Send, 'I'm a battleship. Change course twenty degrees.'" Back came the flashing light, "I'm a lighthouse; advise that you change course." Said Koch, "*We* changed course."[21]

The Gospel of John says of John the Baptist, "He was not the light, but came to bear witness to the light" (RSV). As compelling and as bold as John was, he knew he was not the light himself. Instead, he pointed people, points us still, to the light, even as he advises us to change course.

One of the most human of sins is to think of oneself as the center of things. It is a rather natural assumption from a geographical point of view, someone once said. From where I now sit, to the west is infinity, to the north is infinity, to the east and south, infinity. Same for upward and downward. Thus, I am at the center of things. Other things derive their positions in relationship to me. Parents of small children know that such assumptions describe well the worldview of a two-year-old. It is a normal ethical vantage point for a toddler. Sadly, a lot of people never grow beyond such a stance.[22]

Later in John's Gospel (3:30), John the Baptist will point to Jesus and say, "He must increase, but

I must decrease." By his words and by his self-effacing ministry, John points us toward a stance and a worldview that will prepare our hearts to receive openly the Expected One, just as he did the people who gathered along the banks of the Jordan. It is a helpful reminder to hear him say yet again, "Advise you change course."

Prayer

Reorient our compasses, O God, and point us toward the One who is our light and our life. Amen.

DAY ELEVEN
Reading: Isaiah 11:1–9

At our house and perhaps at yours, this is the time of year when the Christmas wish lists start to appear. Often their appearance is prefaced by some acknowledgment that the entirety of the list is well beyond the family's financial reach, but that if Christmas gifts were to be given this year, any of these items would be nice. "What do you want for Christmas?" is a question frequently asked in this season. And most of us, with any time for thought, can come up with a list.

For some individuals and families, of course, the events of recent months have taken such a toll that a Christmas list seems frivolous, maybe even in bad taste. The normal routine has been rocked by a death, perhaps, or a job loss, or another crisis in the family—and if there were to be a list this year, its contents might only contain a wish for strength or courage or the grace to weather the current upheaval.

When the prophet Isaiah wrote out his vision of his most profound wish list, what scholars and artists have subsequently called "the peaceable

kingdom," his words were shaped by a deep longing for a restored peace, justice, and harmony in
the life of his nation. The people of Judah were in
grave danger, he had warned, for there were
swords rattling beyond their borders (in the
threats of Israel and the gathering power of
Assyria and Egypt) and there were threats from
within (the abuse of power, the neglect of the
poor, the shallowness of faith). Isaiah longed for
the restoration of God's purposes, longed for the
day when the people would find a depth of faith
and lives of faithfulness. With profound elo-
quence, he laid out his vision of God's promise,
that "a shoot shall come out from the stump of
Jesse," that "the spirit of the LORD shall rest on
him," that that leader will usher in a day when
natural and human enemies (wolves and lambs,
calves and lions, nations and nations) will find
peace. "And a little child shall lead them."

That was no small wish list, nor was it his own
best hope alone. It represented Isaiah's understanding of God's fondest hope for God's people.
Particularly because of the reference to the child
who would lead the way to this "peaceable kingdom," Isaiah's vision has become one of our most
cherished Advent texts. Isaiah's hopes are our best

hopes too. Biblical scholar Walter Brueggemann says that the readings of Advent "characterize hope as a visible, public, shared yearning."[23]

Do we know what we want for Christmas this year? Not the little things that will wear out, not the frivolous gifts that will be cast off in time, and not just the gifts that have meaning to us alone, but the gifts of permanence for the whole human family. Do we know what we want? No matter what kind of year we have had, it seems to me that Isaiah's vision offers a wonderful starting place and, one would hope, our ultimate destination.

Prayer

Enlarge our vision of what is possible by Your grace, O God, and so enlarge our hopes. Amen.

DAY TWELVE
Reading: Romans 13:11–14

One of the unexpected pleasures of a summer sabbatical in Europe was riding the remarkable TGV high-speed train across France on our way to Geneva. At speeds approaching two hundred miles per hour, we got a tour of the French countryside that would have made even a New York City cab driver smile. I found it a remarkable irony that the same people who will linger over supper for two or more hours each evening have developed a rail technology that propels trains from town to town at such velocity.

One of the things I noticed as we sped southeast from Paris was that it was nearly impossible to look for long at the rush of the nearer scenery going past the window. Traveling a quarter mile every five seconds or so, one does not have the ability to focus on such things as fence posts and trees and crossing gates. Thus, one learns to take a longer view. Jon Walton once recounted a similar experience and compared it to trying to examine an impressionist painting with one's nose pressed against the canvas. All we see are little dots of color until we stand back and consider the broad scene.[24]

Too often these days life feels like a ride on one of those high-speed trains. Everything seems to happen at high velocity. The workday is one meeting, one task after another in rapid succession. We grab our meals on the run. The kids are involved in too many activities, and time gets squeezed to its limits. And this time of year, with all the parties and gatherings, well—I don't need to rehearse the frenetic pace for anyone. We all know it well.

Paul wrote about time in our passage from Romans: "You know what time it is . . . For salvation is nearer to us now than when we became believers." Paul wrote not just of the passing hours and days. He was standing back and taking a longer view. He was talking of time as that stuff of which a life is made. He was talking of those moments of vision when one pauses long enough to think about where his or her life is heading and maybe, just maybe, even changes course.

One of the lessons my sabbatical summer taught me, one I struggle continually to remember, is that the peace we seek in our lives of stress and toil can only be found if we make peace with time itself, if we carve out of our schedules the time for matters of ultimate consequence—for family and friends, for prayer and reflection, for touching the lives of people who need us (whether we know them or not). Paul says that God is nearer to us than we have ever imagined, already closer than we may ever have hoped. He is saying that time is full of treasure if we will only step back and look. That too is the message of Advent—that the world is full of God if we will only notice. God will come to us again if we will only step back long enough to know what it is we expect.[25]

Prayer

In all the rush and pace of life, O God, enable us to step back to see the gifts of Your goodness all around us. Amen.

DAY THIRTEEN
Reading: Isaiah 64:1–9

Barbara Brown Taylor writes of a visit to the Dingle Peninsula in southwestern Ireland. In the seventh century that rugged coastline was the end of the westernmost point in the known world of the day. Just a few miles off the coast some monks in those days built a monastery at Skellig Michael, a tiny steep rock island named for the archangel. For the better part of seven hundred years they and their followers eked out a bare and spare existence waiting for the return of Christ. They survived the loneliness, the isolation, the sometimes frightful weather, and even a ninth-century assault by the Vikings, who abducted their abbot and starved him to death. Nothing could budge those monks from their rock of vigilance—nothing, that is, until monastic reform arrived in Ireland and less demanding orders of Benedictines and Augustinians began to grow to prominence there. In the thirteenth century, the remaining monks got into their boats and rowed solemnly away from their island outpost forever. Writing of that departure, Taylor observes:

No one knows for sure why they left, but it seems entirely possible to me that they just got tired of waiting. Seven hundred years is a long time to watch the horizon for the coming of the Lord. It is a long time to say your prayers and keep your fasts and live in disciplined community with one another, especially when word reaches you that those on the mainland have made some changes. They are eating better and sleeping later than you are. They have decided they can be in the world a little more without being of it, especially since it looks like they are in for a longer wait than anyone had expected.[26]

For those of us who have made this Advent journey before, we may well look around and wonder if all the waiting and watching is worth it. We look at the world and we wonder what has really changed in all these years. A little progress would be nice, some sense that history is indeed moving forward. But we may wonder. We may even be thinking of readying the boats so we can row away.

The words of Isaiah were a plea for progress but they were more than that; they were a plea for God's intervention. In exile, a long way from home, suffering greatly under the Babylonians,

Isaiah kept his eye on the horizon. He prayed that God would "tear open the heavens and come down, so that the mountains would quake at your presence." Isaiah's cry was for progress and change, a reversal of injustice and a restoration of God's rule. It is still our cry. It is still our hope, even in the face of evidence to the contrary.

Yet we stand with those who have learned to say the name Emmanuel and to claim its meaning, "God with us." And if God is with us, who can possibly stand against us? In a nutshell, that is the hope of Advent, the hope voiced by Isaiah long before the coming of Christ and the hope that has sustained Christ's people from the first Easter until the present age. It is the hope, not so much that God will deliver us from trials, but that God will stand with us and for us in the midst of those trials, that God's justice and mercy will finally prevail, that pain and grief will be redeemed, that our hope will be fulfilled, and that our waiting will not have been in vain.

Prayer

Straining to see the horizon, we may miss Your movement in our midst, O God. Keep us vigilant, but give us eyes to see Your face nearer at hand. Amen.

DAY FOURTEEN

Reading: Luke 1:5–25

Of all the well-worn Christmas stories, one of the least rehearsed is the story of Zechariah and Elizabeth. We have already met their son John, who grew to be known as the Baptist. We know from a bit later in Luke's Gospel that Elizabeth and Mary were kin. But the story of the angel's visit to Zechariah, rich as it is, is often neglected amid all the other familiar stories. That, I believe, is a shame, for there is much in this story with which we could well identify.

Zechariah and Elizabeth were not a young couple. They were, in fact, well past their childbearing and child-raising years when the angel of the Lord came to Zechariah to tell him that Elizabeth was to have a child. In a scene reminiscent of the mysterious visitation of three strangers to Abraham and Sarah, the angel announces the long-awaited news to Zechariah and elaborates with detail the kind of Spirit-filled life their son will lead. "You will have joy and gladness," he says to the stricken Zechariah, "and many will rejoice." But Zechariah is skeptical.

"How will I know that this is so?" he asks. "For I am an old man, and my wife is getting on in years." The angel responds with authority ("I am Gabriel. I stand in the presence of God") and with punishment for Zechariah's skepticism ("Because you did not believe my words . . . you will become mute, unable to speak, until the day these things occur").

Barbara Brown Taylor calls Zechariah "the patron saint of the twenty-first-century church":

The commentaries call Zechariah's question the sin of disbelief, but I wonder about that. You might also call it a failure of imagination, a fear of disappointment, a habit of hopelessness. He had waited a long time for something that was systematically denied him. He had gotten used to not being heard. . . .

Like [Zechariah] we have been waiting a long time for our prayers to be heard. "Christ has died. Christ is risen. Christ will come again," we say over and over again. But where is he, exactly, and how much longer must we wait? It is hard to know what to say when people ask us where God is. Have faith? Be patient? Prayer works? Our words have gotten as old and tired as we have, and in many cases people have stopped believing us. They ask us the same thing Zechariah asked his angel. "How will we know that this is so?" Maybe it is time for us to claim the angel's gift of silence again—to stop talking so much, to stop trying to explain, to shut our mouths before the terrible mystery of God and see what the quiet has to teach us.[27]

Kathleen Norris adds a thought about Zechariah that also speaks to our impatience and our tendency always to want explanations: "I read Zechariah's punishment as a grace, in that he could not say anything to further compound his initial arrogance when confronted with mystery. When he does speak again, it is to praise God; he's had nine months to think it over."[28] In a cacophony of noise from every direction, the gift of silence these days may be a grace indeed! So in Advent we sing, "Let all mortal flesh keep silence."

Prayer

Help us in these days, O God, to be silent before the mystery of this season, and thus to listen for the angel's promise. Amen.

DAY FIFTEEN *(Third Sunday of Advent)*
Reading: John 1:19–34

John the Baptist reappears on the Third Sunday of Advent, this time not screaming out a call for major change, but fending off speculation that he himself might be the Messiah. It is easy to understand why some people might have thought so. But John is adamant. He is not the Christ. He is not Elijah. He is not the prophet. He is merely the one to point to the Messiah. Upon spotting Jesus, he says, "Look, here is the Lamb of God!" John points away from himself, when all eyes are on him, to make certain that the people's focus is where it should be.

In a nutshell, John defines the role of the Christian church and the role of all faithful Christian people. We are to point to the Christ. Our worship, our outreach and compassion to people in need, and our demonstrations of faithfulness are never ends in themselves but means of pointing to the Lamb.

A good friend introduced me a few years ago to a Japanese proverb that says, "The finger points to the moon. Woe to the one who confuses the finger with the moon."[29] In a conversation with a local resident about all the construction going on at the churches in recent years in the town where I live, I was asked why churches invest so much money in steeples. Couldn't the money invested in such structures be better spent on the needs of people? Similar questions were part of the discussion also during the rebuilding of the church I serve after a terrible fire in 1958 destroyed its buildings. The church needs to invest itself in human need, but the steeple, like the ministry of the church, is also valuable because of the One to whom it points, stretching out toward eternity. Of course, there may sometimes be a temptation to confuse the finger with the moon, to confuse the church with the One to whom it points. When that happens, we have forgotten our purpose.

In Matthias Grünewald's artistic masterpiece, the Isenheim Altarpiece, the central panel depicts the crucifixion. Unlike some renderings of that scene in which the Christ is portrayed as the picture of serenity, the Grünewald crucifixion is painfully grotesque in its contrast of light and darkness. Here the suffering Jesus is harrowingly detailed, a twisted and bloody figure. The suffering Christ is the central focus, gaunt and bleeding. To one side, the German painter has added the Madonna being comforted by John the Apostle and Mary Magdalene, and to the right, as a secondary focal point in the painting, John the Baptist and a lamb. John's arm is outstretched, and his crudely elongated index finger points to the cross. Just below, Grünewald has inscribed the Baptist's words from John 3:30: "He must increase, but I must decrease."

There was no chance that John would confuse the finger with the moon, nor himself with the One he came to serve. In our Advent journey, part of the discipline we seek to learn is the discipline of deflecting and reflecting the light from ourselves to the One who is the light of the world.

Prayer

We who live in shadows stand in need of Your light, O God, and so to You we point with our hands and hearts and voices. Amen.

DAY SIXTEEN

Reading: 1 Thessalonians 5:16–24

Paul's closing exhortations to the Thessalonians are familiar words, though admittedly difficult to employ: "Rejoice always, pray without ceasing, give thanks in all circumstances." In the context of Advent, when one thinks about preparation and a life of expectation, one can understand why these words are part of the lectionary. But there is also another reason to consider this text in these days. This is a season when we celebrate the "Word made flesh," what theologians call the "incarnation," when the eternal God chose to be revealed in human form. In a related way, Paul's words to the Thessalonians dwell upon the incarnation of Christian life and faith, the "fleshing out" of all that we say and believe about the Christ. Paul reminds the Thessalonians that faithful people are called to live out their faith in active ways, and he does so with aphorisms so profoundly simple that we may miss their depth.[30]

Simply put, if we expect Jesus' return, that expectation will show itself in the faithful living of our lives. And as it does, we may find ourselves surprised by the fruit of such living. Pastor Ted Wardlaw describes an Advent Communion service several years ago with his congregation in Atlanta. On that Sunday, the elements were to be received by intinction, with the congregation coming forward to take a piece of bread and dip it in the cup. As in many churches where the sacrament is so shared, it is the custom of his congregation to share words such as "the body of Christ" and "the cup of salvation" as the elements are presented. But before the service began, one of the elders suggested using Paul's word "Rejoice!" as a preface to the customary phrases. "It may help," he said. "After all, it often seems that folks come forward as though they were about to consume hemlock."

So they agreed to add the word: "Rejoice! The body of Christ." Wardlaw said he pondered the difference the word might make as the congregation lined up to receive the elements. The thought became almost overwhelming as he looked into the faces of those people—one recuperating from open-heart surgery, another feebly walking with a cane, another whose child had been killed in an accident, a couple trying to hold a troubled marriage together. But he spoke the words of blessing and exhortation. "Rejoice, Allan. . . . Rejoice, Mary. . . ." As he did, he could see amid the smiles and tears of response something of what the apostle Paul must have known when he said, "Rejoice always." For days and weeks afterward, Wardlaw said, thinking of that service nuanced the way he interacted with everyone he met.[31]

Are we those who expect Christ's reign and rule in the world, in our lives? Then we shall know how to live in the meantime. We shall know how to rejoice.

Prayer

Give us, O God, hearts for rejoicing, ceaseless prayers for voicing, and hearts of deepening gratitude for Your great love, made known to us in Jesus Christ. Amen.

DAY SEVENTEEN
Reading: Matthew 11:2–11

What kind of Christ do we expect? That seems to be the issue behind the delegation of John the Baptist's followers coming to inquire if Jesus was indeed the Expected One. Perhaps John wanted Jesus to be, well, more fiery, more assertive. John, after all, had preached about repentance and the reordering of life, and Jesus seemed to be welcoming those whom John despised. (Our expectations of Jesus often keep us from seeing the real Jesus.) And so Jesus sent John's friends back to John, now in prison, and told them to tell John what they had seen and heard—the blind receive sight, the lame walk, lepers are cured, the dead are raised, and the poor have good news preached to them. That's who I am and what I am about, Jesus says.

But again, what kind of Christ do *we* expect? What kind of Jesus do we want? One who blesses our ambition and cheers our cunning? One who approves our competitive, acquisitive, even self-centered ways? Given the way our culture celebrates the season, one would certainly assume the Christ we worship is part of the ethos of the ever more expensive toys and gifts we purchase.

New Testament scholar Luke Timothy Johnson, who teaches at Emory University's Candler School of Theology, tells of going Christmas shopping a few years ago at Lenox Square, one of Atlanta's largest shopping malls. There, amid all the lights and all the displays and all the rush of shoppers, Johnson says he was suddenly overcome by a need to escape. "I all of a sudden was struck," he says, "there is nothing in this place that anybody really needs; and furthermore, nothing anyone really needs is in this place."[32]

Into the often heated competition between wants and needs, Jesus comes to refocus our energies and to claim our hearts. The things we need are safety, shelter, healing, meaning, and purpose. "Go and tell John what you hear and see," he says. All the rest is window dressing, despite the fact that we spend so much of our time, energy, and resources on such things.

Some months ago I heard an encouraging report on National Public Radio that a substantial and growing number of the best and the brightest of our college and university students are planning to devote their lives to teaching. By conscious choice, said the report, these young adults are eschewing the better salaries and the more affluent lifestyles afforded by corporate America in order to focus on a matter of great consequence. Often they are students who have grown up in affluent families but they hunger still, not for more things but for something more important—a sense of purpose in life.

This month, amid all the shopping, maybe we can take time to ask what our friends and family members really need, and what *we* really need—what our deepest hungers are. And as a gift, both to ourselves and others, we might commit ourselves to living into a future where those needs and hungers are met. Along the way of such a pilgrimage we may well meet the Christ—the One we need, if not always the one we want.

Prayer
It is a difficult season for sorting out needs and wants, gracious God, but stay with us, we pray, and show us the way to wholeness and peace. Amen.

DAY EIGHTEEN

Reading: John 1:1–5

On a recent summer visit to the library of the university near where I live, I discovered some of the poems of Cambridge professor Geoffrey Hill. In one of his poems, "Christmas Trees," Hill remembers the imprisonment of German pastor Dietrich Bonhoeffer, who paid with his life for his opposition to Hitler. The young pastor was in prison as Christmas arrived in 1943.

> "Bonhoeffer in his skylit cell
> bleached by the flares' candescent fall . . ."[33]

The poem is one of encouragement, inspiration, and challenge. However one understands the legacy of Dietrich Bonhoeffer, the poet reminds us that Christmas comes not only into the gaiety of the season but also into the darkest and most difficult circumstances. The promise of Advent and Christmas, as voiced by John's Gospel, is that the darkness, in whatever form it takes, will never prevail against the light Christ brings.

More than a few times at Christmas Eve services I have shared with congregations Bonhoeffer's extraordinary letter to his parents that Christmas. Remarkably, he wrote not of the darkness of the experience, but of the peace that surrounded him:

Of course you can't help thinking of my being in prison over Christmas, and it is bound to throw a shadow over the few hours of happiness which still await you in these times. All I can do to help is to assure you that I know you will keep it in the same spirit as I do, for we are agreed on how Christmas ought to be kept. How could it be otherwise when my attitude toward Christmas is a heritage I owe to you? I need not tell you how much I long to be released and to see you all again. But for years you have given us such lovely Christmases, that our grateful memories are strong enough to cast their rays over a darker one. *In times like these we learn as never before what it means to possess a past and a spiritual heritage untrammeled by the changes and chances of the present.* A spiritual heritage reaching back for centuries is a wonderful support and comfort in the face of all temporary stresses and strains. . . .

For a Christian there is nothing peculiarly difficult about Christmas in a prison cell. I daresay it will have more meaning and will be observed with greater sincerity here in this prison than in places where all that survives of the feast is its name. That misery, suffering, poverty, loneliness, helplessness look very different to the eyes of God from what they do to [human eyes], that God should come down to the very place which [mortals] usually abhor, that Christ was born in a stable because there was no room for him in the inn—these are things which a prisoner can understand better than anyone else. For [us] the Christmas story is glad tidings in a very real sense. And that faith gives [us] a part in the communion of saints, a fellowship transcending the bounds of time and space and reducing the months of confinement here to insignificance.[34]

"The light shines in the darkness," wrote John, "and the darkness has not overcome it" (RSV).

Prayer
In seasons of light and in seasons of darkness, we give You thanks for Your unquenchable light, O God. Shine it upon our hearts, we pray. Amen.

DAY NINETEEN

Reading: Luke 12:13–21

The parable of the rich fool is not usually associated with Advent; it is more often pulled out during stewardship season. But there is a deep sense in which Advent is very much about stewardship, particularly the stewardship of time. Are we serious about the way we prepare in these days, or are we more cavalier in our time-consciousness, like the rich fool? Are we ready to receive the One who comes, or are we consumed with our own concerns and strivings, even those of a religious nature? If the reader will indulge one more poem by Geoffrey Hill, it seems to me that his "Lachrimae Amantis" speaks eloquently to this theme. The writer speaks of "the angel of my house" who whispers to him in his dreams:

"your lord is coming, he is close" . . .
"tomorrow I shall wake to welcome him."[35]

Tomorrow. Where is the resolve for this morning or this night? Where is the heart that will claim Christ's coming now and act for all the world as though He has already come? Where is the will to take seriously a Word that we have relegated to the liturgies and sentiments of the season? The parable, like the poem, is a powerful reminder of the claim God makes on us and His constraints upon our conditional promises of "tomorrow." The Lord wants today. This day. Now.

Prayer

To us who would protect ourselves against Your claim, eternal God, to us who expect nothing but delay, stir us with Your promises yet again, that we may seize this day as Your day. Amen.

DAY TWENTY
Reading: Philippians 2:5–11

These days one can find fairly frequent radio and television broadcasts of some of the great Christmas musical repertoire, everything from the familiar lessons and carols service at King's College to Handel's *Messiah*, and seasonal classics from Charles Gounod, Pietro Yon, and others. Music plays such an important part in this season.

While thinking about the sacred songs that give meaning to the church's life in these days, I was reminded of a story about one of my old teachers at Yale Divinity School, George Lindbeck, a giant of a theologian. Yale professor and friend David Bartlett shared with me his remembrance of Lindbeck's retirement party at the divinity school a few years back.

> It was Christmastime and, as it happened, George had only recently come home from the hospital where he had undergone surgery. After the appreciative speeches, when it was time for George to make his remarks, he said this: "Last week in the hospital I was listening to the radio and heard the annual Christmas

concert from St. Olaf College. During the intermission the announcer asked one of the choir members why she took such obvious delight in singing in the choir. She replied, 'When I sing I become part of a song that began long before I arrived here and will continue long after I am gone.' When I do Christian theology, I become part of a song that began long before I arrived here and will continue long after I have gone."[36]

Stepping into Advent and Christmas each year, I am struck by something of the same continuity of tradition and meaning. I am part of a company of watchers and waiters whose melodies have preceded me by generations, melodies that, God willing, will continue to echo long after I am gone. Nowhere do I experience that legacy more fully than in the liturgical visit we pay each year to the texts and tunes of the season. As we think about the One who is to come, it draws me into the story more deeply to sing once more that twelfth-century Latin text, "O Come, O Come, Emmanuel," or Charles Wesley's eighteenth-century hymn, "Come, Thou Long-Expected Jesus." It startles me to sing Philipp Nicolai's "Sleepers, Wake!" to the harmonies of J. S. Bach. And as we approach

Christmas I never tire of the running "glorias" of the French carol, "Angels We Have Heard on High." I never get weary as the lights in our sanctuary are brought down to Joseph Mohr's "Silent Night" or back up to Isaac Watts's triumphant "Joy to the World!" Over the years, new hymns have come along to add luster and meaning to this season of light, and to echo the early Christ hymn recorded by the apostle Paul so many years ago in our reading from Philippians.

We are part of a song that began long before we arrived here and that will continue long after we are gone. In the meantime, it is our privilege to lend our voices and hearts to the celebration of its wonderful melody and message.

Prayer

Tune our hearts to sing Your praise, O God, that we may lift our voices in grateful and joyful celebration of the One who comes. Amen.

DAY TWENTY-ONE

Reading: Isaiah 9:2–7

Music is much on my mind as this week comes to a close, in part because tomorrow the choirs of many churches will stir congregations once again with their annual presentations of the music of Christmas. Such music feeds the soul and lifts the heart. I have been grateful for that gift for years in the churches I have served, and my sabbatical summer of worship in other churches only served to extend my gratitude for those in every congregation who lend their talents, voices, and hearts to the church's worship week after week. Music is such an important part of the worship of God's people.

I have also thought about how music has shaped our hearing and understanding of the scriptures, particularly the texts of Advent. This passage from Isaiah is no exception. I have read Isaiah's vision of restoration and hope so many times, but for years I have not been able to read it without hearing the solitary voice and then the chorus of Handel's *Messiah*. The single voice belongs to the bass soloist, with the prophetic recitative: "The people that walked in darkness have seen a great light; and they that dwell in the land of the shadow of death, upon them hath the light shined." The music is gracious good news to all who have known the trials of their own particular exiles, just as Isaiah's words were balm and hope for his people. But the chorus that follows seals the promise with a particular vision of God's coming reign, a vision we claim yet again in this season of the year: "For unto us a child is born, unto us a son is given: and the government shall be upon his shoulder; and his name shall be called Wonderful, Counsellor, The mighty God, The everlasting Father, The Prince of Peace."

It is more than just nice music for this season of light and hope. These words have afforded enough light to see through some of the darkest days of human history; they are words that stir in us blessed memories of God's goodness and a foundation of hope for the new thing that God is yet doing among us. We believe the expected "child" of Isaiah's prophecy was born of Mary in the darkness and cold and that the light that shone on and within the stable of his birth has never been extinguished.

In the dark moments of deep uncertainty, of

profound loneliness, of tormenting grief—in the deep darkness of whatever life throws at us, the voice of that bass soloist and the bold response from the chorus echoing Isaiah can afford us precious comfort and peace, and encouragement enough to face the days ahead. The season of Advent reminds us that Christmas is not about happiness but joy, about the death of fear, about the transformation of human hope. Nowhere do I hear that message more profoundly than through the glorious music of these days—echoes, I think, of the angels' song.

Prayer

You know the songs that sing themselves within the depths of our hearts, gracious God. We thank You for the music that stirs us so. Amen.

DAY TWENTY-TWO (*Fourth Sunday of Advent*)

Reading: Luke 1:26–38

I have tried to imagine the moment. Was there a knock on the door? Did the angel make any inquiries around Nazareth about Mary? Did he just appear next to her, scaring her half to death with his "Greetings!" or "Hail, favored one" or whatever it was he said before he said, "The Lord is with you"? I love the understatement of the biblical account: "[Mary] was greatly troubled at the saying" (RSV). I'll bet she was troubled!

Our reading today is known as "the annunciation." Over the centuries, the moment of Gabriel's visit to Mary, the remarkable announcement, and the words Mary and the angel exchange have been the subjects of artistic interpretations in music, poetry, painting, and sculpture. This most improbable of encounters is, the church contends, a watershed moment in human history, as the angel speaks of God's outrageous plan and awaits the answer of the teenaged girl.

Her initial response is understandably hesitant and halting. "How can this be?" she asks. Examining that moment, Barbara Brown Taylor says that there are several other questions she might have asked. For example:

Will Joseph stick around? Will my parents still love me? Will my friends stand by me or will I get dragged into town and stoned for sleeping around? Will the pregnancy go all right? Will the labor be hard? Will there be someone there to help me when my time comes? Will I know what to do? You say the child will be king of Israel, but what about me? Will I survive his birth? What about me?[37]

But Mary asks none of those questions, and ultimately her response is one of exemplary faith. This encounter between Gabriel and Mary, says Kathleen Norris, is a moment when "hope contends with fear," a moment of significance for all of us and each of us:

Gabriel addresses his majestic words in an unlikely setting to an unlikely person, someone poor and powerless, extremely vulnerable in her place and time, a young peasant woman about to find herself pregnant before her wedding. But if the angel's words express the hopes of generations of Israel, Mary's response is silence. The angel spells out the wonders that are about to ensue, again in exalted terms: Mary's son will be a king whose kingdom has no end. "How can this be?" Mary exclaims, finally, and the angel says, "The power of the Most High will overshadow you; *therefore* the child will be called Son of God." Mary says very little, and she says it simply: "Here am I," and "let it be."

The angel's "therefore" seems alarmingly significant, the seed of what Christian theologians have for well over a thousand years termed the scandal of the Incarnation. It also resonates with my own life. When a place or time seems touched by God, it is an overshadowing, a sudden eclipsing of my priorities and plans. But even in terrible circumstances and calamities, in matters of life and death, if I sense that I am in the shadow of God, I find light, so much light that my vision improves dramatically. I know that holiness is near.

And it is not robed in majesty. It does not assert itself with the raw power of empire (not even the little empire of self in which I all too often reside), but it waits in puzzlement, it hesitates. Coming from Galilee, as it were, from a place of little hope, it reveals

the ordinary circumstances of my life to be
full of mystery, and gospel, which means
"good news."[38]

Prayer

*Help us to claim not only the ancient truth of an
encounter long ago, O God, but also the reality of
Your encounters with us this day, that we, like
Mary, may respond with trust. Amen.*

DAY TWENTY-THREE

Reading: Matthew 1:18–25

In the Christmas pageant scene in John Irving's *A Prayer for Owen Meany*, John Wheelwright says, "What an uninspiring role it is, to be Joseph—that hapless follower, that stand-in, that guy along for the ride."[39] Joseph is often dismissed and disregarded in the playing of the Christmas pageants, in part because he is misunderstood. Pastor Linda Loving tells of a conversation involving her sister and her four-year-old niece, Megan.

> It was a few days before Christmas and Megan, four, was drawing a picture of the nativity. When she completed her work she explained each character to her mother: shepherds and sheep, three Wise Men and camels, the stable with cows and a cat and a dog and the manger and, of course, Mary and the baby. Megan's mother . . . noticed that someone was missing. . . . "Where's Joseph?" she asked innocently, assuming, of course, that Megan would remember and sketch him in. Slightly exasperated, [Megan] shot back decisively, "Who needs Joseph anyway?"[40]

Megan's sentiments, like John Wheelwright's, are probably shared by a lot of folks who can't quite figure how Joseph fits into this story.

My reading of Matthew's account of Joseph, however, is more sympathetic to Joseph. As I see it, Joseph has a very important role to play in the drama unfolding in Nazareth. Learning of Mary's pregnancy, he holds her future, and by implication, the future of humankind, in his hands. One preacher says, "If Joseph believes the angel, everything is on. The story can continue. . . . But if Joseph does not believe, then everything grinds to a halt. If he wakes up from his dream, shakes his head, and goes on to the courthouse to file the divorce papers, then Mary is an outcast forever."[41]

But Joseph is caught in a moral dilemma. Luke describes him as "a righteous man." Mary's word to him that she is pregnant would seem to call for a prescribed course of action. But the angel in the dream insists that the pregnancy is part of God's plan. What is he to do? In his Christmas oratorio, *For the Time Being*, poet W. H. Auden hears Joseph plead with the angel:

"All I ask is one
Important and elegant proof . . ."[42]

He wants to know that this is all God's doing. But there is no proof, only the angel's word. Conventional righteousness would seem to require Joseph to dismiss Mary—it was, after all, a just cause. The angel, on the other hand, calls him to embrace the new thing God is doing. As Tom Long says, "Being righteous is never simply being pure and good in the abstract; genuine righteousness is always joining with God to do God's work in the world."[43] By grace, Joseph chooses the path of creative righteousness in partnership with God.

What are we to make of these two remarkable encounters with the angel—Mary's first and now Joseph's? I like the way my friend Rick Spalding puts it:

> [W]hat began as a project of planning the ordinariness of a couple of lives tied together . . . turns out to be a project of making room for the life of God in the midst of the structures, the plans and the patterns. Mary and Joseph are the great-grandparents of the dislocation of our well-drawn maps. They are the patron saints of our own scrambling to accommodate the will of God as a demanding newborn in the straw of our ordinary days. Who knows if we will rise to this interruption

with the grace of quiet resolve, the wit of a fer-
tile imagination—or whether we will rail
against it with every ounce of ordinariness we
have?[44]

Prayer
Amid all the patterned responses we have
devised and cherished, help us yet to be open to
the new things You are doing and to the parts
You want us to play, O God, our creator. Amen.

DAY TWENTY-FOUR

Reading: Luke 1:46–55

In Dorothy Sayers's Christmas play, *Kings in Judea*, the Magi visit Mary and converse with her for a while before they present their lavish gifts to the Christ-child. They seem concerned about the nature of power in this conversation, until finally Mary speaks:

> When the Angel's message came to me, the Lord put a song into my heart. I suddenly saw that wealth and cleverness were nothing to God—no one is too unimportant to be His friend. That was the thought that came to me, because of the thing that happened to *me*. I am quite humbly born, yet the Power of God came upon me; very foolish and unlearned, yet the Word of God was spoken to me; and I was in deep distress, when my Baby was born and filled my life with love. So I know very well that Wisdom and Power and Sorrow *can* live together with Love; and for me, the Child in my arms is the answer to all the riddles.[45]

Luke's understanding of Mary and Sayers's portrayal both hinge on the powerful reversal at work in the birth of the Christ. Nowhere do we sense that reversal more powerfully than in the song the Lord put in Mary's heart, what the church has traditionally called the Magnificat (after its initial Latin word). It is a song that begins with a mood appropriate to the season: "My soul magnifies the Lord, and my spirit rejoices in God my Savior, for he has regarded the low estate of his handmaiden" (RSV). It begins as a song of gratitude and humility, but there is more. As William Barclay said, "There is a loveliness in the *Magnificat,* but in that loveliness there is dynamite."[46] What follows is a prophetic song (voiced in what biblical scholars call "prophetic perfect" tense—it anticipates an action, but announces it as already accomplished) that describes the great reversal of fortunes begun at Bethlehem. God, Mary sings,

> has shown strength with his arm,
> he has scattered the proud in the imagination of
>   their hearts,
> he has put down the mighty from their thrones,
> and exalted those of low degree;
> he has filled the hungry with good things,
> and the rich he has sent empty away. (RSV)

Our perspective shapes the way we hear and

receive this word and determines how forcefully we add our voices to her chorus. That Mary's song was and is good news for a great many is indisputable; that it strikes others as revolutionary is similarly beyond doubt. The most important matter for the present moment is how we shall respond to the Magnificat. What we understand about Mary's child will have a lot to do with how we understand ourselves, and those understandings will shape and guide the way we understand and interact with others—whether of high or low degree, whether rich or poor, whether powerful or wholly lacking in power. Throughout Luke's Gospel it is clear that Jesus has a special affinity for the poor, for those driven to the margins. Our first sign is Mary's song. Living as many of us do in communities that seem to be increasingly uncomfortable with the poor among us, we would do well to hear that song again.

Prayer

Do not let us turn our ears from Mary's song, O God, nor let us turn our hearts from those whom Jesus loved so tenderly. Amen.

DAY TWENTY-FIVE

Reading: Romans 16:25–27

Has Christmas gotten out of hand? Is it too big? Someone asked me those questions last year a few days before Christmas. The easy answer, of course, is yes—at least commercially, at least in the way we try to celebrate it too much of the time. But if we read Paul's closing words from his letter to the Romans, we would have to say that the problem with our Christmas celebrations is that we have thought of Christmas in terms too small. Too often Christmas gets reduced to custom and repetitive ritual, to wish lists and parties and "what did you get?" We need to remember its cosmic importance. We need to contemplate the great gift we have been given. Such a realization brings to mind one of my favorite poems of Ann Weems:

> What do I want for Christmas?
> I want to kneel in Bethlehem,
>   the air thick with alleluias,
>   the angels singing
>   that God is born among us.
> In the light of the Star
>   I want to see them come,
>   the wise ones and the humble.

I want to see them come
    bearing whatever they treasure
        to lay at the feet
            of him who gives his life.

What do I want for Christmas?
To see in that stable
    the whole world kneeling in thanks
        for a promise kept;
            new life.
For in his nativity
    we find ours.[47]

Has Christmas gotten out of hand? Is it too big? On the contrary, in many ways it is the victim of a smallness of heart and hope. Having accustomed ourselves to the customary, we have perhaps missed something very important. Says my friend Jon Walton, "It is so easy to write a script for our lives, to become so fixed on how we will expect things will be that we close ourselves off from the surprising and the unexpected."[48] God is at work in these days. These are days of hope and promise. All we have to do is open ourselves to the powerful new thing God is doing.

Prayer

For all Your surprising goodness to us, we will live this day in joy and praise, holy God. Awaken us to Your presence and work among us now. Amen.

DAY TWENTY-SIX
Reading: Luke 2:1–4

Over the centuries what happened at Bethlehem has inspired some of the greatest treasures of Western art. Of all those paintings and sculptures, there is one that has continued to engage my heart and imagination over the last couple of decades. It is Pieter Brueghel's painting, *The Numbering at Bethlehem*. In the early seventeenth century, the Flemish painter depicted the first verses of Luke's Gospel not by trying to envision the ancient Bethlehem but by portraying it as a typical Flemish village of his day. Snow is on the ground in Brueghel's Bethlehem, its soft white contrasting with the browns all around. The village ponds are frozen over, and children frolic on the ice as the other villagers go about their daily chores. Handcarts of goods are parked in front of the local inn, where a crowd has gathered. A Christmas wreath hangs on the wall of the inn, the only hint that this winter day holds any special meaning. Almost lost in all the activity in the painting, in the right-center foreground a man carrying a saw is approaching the inn, with a donkey and its rider, a young woman, in tow. Nearly lost in the scene, Mary and Joseph have been captured by Brueghel as they make their way to the inn to be registered in the census. Just an ordinary day in an ordinary town.[49]

Brueghel's painting has been a powerful reminder to me of the simple truth that Jesus was born not into glory and grandeur but into humble simplicity. This is the child who grew in wisdom, and part of the wisdom He claimed is that there is extraordinary value in people who live the most ordinary of lives. That is why those of us who claim His name need regularly to remind ourselves of the ministry of grace and hospitality He has entrusted to us. In the name of One born in a stable because there was no room for Him in that village inn, we are to live with a passion for compassion and hospitality.

Some years ago, my friend Joanna Adams told the story of a young advertising executive in the church she was then serving who showed up every week as a volunteer in the church's shelter for homeless persons in one of the South's largest cities. In appearance, she said, the young man was right out of *GQ* magazine, but in his capacity for compassion, he was second only to the heart of God. Joanna asked him once why he came back every week, and he said the most amazing thing: "I figured Jesus meant what he said in the twenty-fifth chapter of Matthew [about ministering to the 'least of these']. I figure I stand the best chance I've got in these days of encountering the spirit of Christ here. . . . Besides, these guys and I are not all that different. They wear their brokenness on the outside. I wear mine on the inside. But brokenness is brokenness. It is the condition we share."[50] He might well have added that it was the circumstance into which and for which Christ was born.

The good news of Christmas is not a gift to be hoarded; it is meant to be shared. It needs to be offered as our gift to all, not just in words but also in deeds. As Scottish preacher Kathy Galloway says, "The Word became flesh, not more words. It lived among us."[51] Preacher, poet, and songwriter John Bell of the Iona Community says it this way:

Pull back the curtain on Bethlehem's stable.
Strip off the tinsel and peer through the dark.
Look at the child who's a threat, yet in danger,

homeless and helpless he first makes his mark. Love is the secret, love is the secret. Love is God's cradle, God's table, God's cup and God's ark.[52]

Prayer

Do not let us hide at the manger, O God, or blend into the ordinariness of our daily lives, but shape our hearts that we might take forth the joy, love, and welcome of the angels into all the world. Amen.

CHRISTMAS EVE

Reading: Luke 2:1–20

It was an unexpected Christmas Eve surprise. The snow had been falling most of the day along the coast of South Carolina, and Charleston was blanketed with some eight inches of snow. We were going to have a white Christmas just four months after the destruction of Hurricane Hugo. The roads and bridges were getting icy, so we decided to play it safe and cancel the 11 P.M. candlelight service. But we shoveled the steps and sidewalks for the 7:30 P.M. service and welcomed a surprisingly large congregation, ready to sing and speak of shepherds and mangers and the good news of Bethlehem.

I was preaching when it happened. I don't remember what I was saying (I'm fairly confident that Luke's second chapter was the text), but I was in the pulpit when I saw the door at the rear of the center aisle open. A man stepped in, carrying a sack of some sort, and took a seat in one of the folding chairs set up behind the back pew. The church was a suburban congregation, but it sat on a major highway, and so we did have folks stop by on their way from one place to another. I didn't think much of it. But after the service, after we had sung "Joy to the World!" and made our way out into the December cold, one of our elders came over and said there was a gentleman in the church office who wanted to speak to me.

The man was probably fifty years old, a seaman just off a ship that had docked a few hours earlier in Charleston harbor. He had walked out from downtown, trying to make his way through the snow to North Charleston, he said, when he saw the lights and heard the singing from inside the church. He said he didn't need money; he simply needed a place to stay for a couple of days. Immediately I began trying to think of what options might be available at that hour on a snowy night when most everything in the city was closed. But he quickly went on to say that he had an old Navy friend who lived in North Charleston (across the icy bridge, of course). He remembered only his friend's first name, so he had no way to make a telephone call, but he remembered where he lived, and he thought if someone could just give him a ride, the friend would take care of the rest.

I was skeptical that this "friend" was going to welcome this man into his home on Christmas Eve without any advance notice, but I agreed to take him to his friend's house. We turned off the lights of the church, got into my Honda, and started off toward the North Bridge. The bridge was indeed a bit slick, but we made it across, and we reached the neighborhood in less than twenty minutes. After a few trips around the block while he checked and rechecked his memory, the man pointed to a house, and I pulled over. He left his duffel bag in the back seat and walked up to the front porch. It was a simple, whitewashed, concrete-block house. There was a light on, but I couldn't help but wonder if it was the right house or, if it was, if the friend still lived there anyway. Just the same, he knocked on the door. It opened, with the chain still in place, and through it I could see a woman's face. My passenger spoke to the woman for a minute, and then she closed the door. I figured he had it wrong—that it was the wrong house, or his friend had moved—but a moment later the door opened again, and this time a big man, strong-shouldered and mustached, ex-tended his hand to the man and put his left hand on my passenger's shoulder. Then they embraced. The big man smiled, then called for the woman, and the three of them stood at the door for a few moments. A moment later my passenger was back at the car. "He got married since I saw him last," he said, "but his wife said it would be okay, so I think everything is fine. I really do appreciate all your trouble." And with that, he was off.

But it wasn't trouble, really. In fact, it was the most extraordinary gift—to find someone with such confidence in an old friend's hospitality and a friend who was willing to take in an unexpected and uninvited guest on Christmas Eve. Beyond everything I could have remembered about that white Christmas, those two men standing on the porch are my most enduring memory. That night Christmas Eve truly seemed to be what a friend calls it: "the night when all heaven breaks loose."

Born in the night, Mary's Child,
  A long way from Your home;
Coming in need, Mary's Child,
  Born in a borrowed room.
Clear shining light, Mary's Child,
  Your face lights up our way;
Light of the world, Mary's Child,
  Dawn on our darkened day.[53]

Prayer

Our prayer this day, O God, is as simple and unadorned as the birth we celebrate: Show us the meaning of Christmas, so that our hearts may be full of joy and our lives may be full of grace. Amen.

CHRISTMAS DAY

Reading: John 1:1–14

Sometimes new metaphors illuminate old words.
I remember the first time I heard North Carolina
singer-songwriter David Wilcox in concert at an
arts center near our home. At the outset the
music was playful, light, and tender. There were
love songs that seemed to capture the language of
the heart. He sang a song about an old car and
another about celebrating a thirtieth birthday on
a roller coaster. Then at the beginning of his second set, he sang his song, "Show the Way." Serious and spiritual in its content and powerful in its
imagery, the song is a testament of hope in the
midst of everything that calls for hopelessness.
Wilcox challenges hearers who see only darkness,
and thus who see the triumph of evil in the world,
to consider the design God has on this life. The
song's chorus reminds the listener of the great
drama of life and redemption at the heart of the
Christmas message.

> It is love who makes the mortar
> And it's love who stacked these stones
> And it's love who made the stage here

Although it looks like we're alone
In this scene set in shadows
Like the night is here to stay
There is evil cast around us
But it's love that wrote the play
And in this darkness love can show the way.[54]

Wilcox has found another metaphor to underscore the promise of the Prologue to John that "the light shines in the darkness, and the darkness has not overcome it" (RSV). This is what we celebrate this Christmas Day. We do not claim that the darkness is gone or that there is no evil or suffering or hardship in this world; to do so would be to fly in the face of our experience of the world. No, but we do claim that the light that first shone on Bethlehem shines still, that the light and love of God set loose in that manger hold the ultimate power and are our final destination. Even in the darkness, that "love can show the way."

The journey of Christian faith and discipleship does not end at Christmas. It begins here. Our watching and wakefulness are not now accomplished because Christmas has come. We still keep our eyes on the horizon. We still change course when we feel impelled to do so. We still watch and listen for signs of God's promised presence, even as we give thanks that the Word became flesh and dwelt among us. That Word abides with us still. "Joy to the world! the Lord is come."

Prayer

As You first came to dwell with humankind so many years ago, come again to dwell in our hearts and hopes this day, this Christmas Day. Amen.

THE DAY AFTER CHRISTMAS

Reading: Matthew 2:1–12

This is not the best day to read the story of the visit of the Magi; its reading belongs more appropriately to the day of Epiphany (January 6), which celebrates their visit. But I have chosen it as the concluding text for this devotional guide because of its emphasis on the gifts we bring to Christ, which I see as a healthy counterpoint to the ethos of gift-getting we have all experienced in recent days. I remember another who came with a gift of her own on this day some years ago—Will Campbell's Grandma Bettye:

> And she wore the flannel bathrobe to church
> the very first Sunday after Christmas.
> Because it was the prettiest thing she
>   had ever seen,
>   and the Lord deserved the best.
> And because it was 1933, and she didn't have a
>   bathroom.[55]

I remember Campbell's Grandma Bettye every year on the Sunday after Christmas. I think of her at some point each year in the shopping season that precedes Christmas too, because almost every year there is some "have to have" toy that parents are madly rushing about to find for their children: Beanie Babies all the way back to Cabbage Patch dolls. One year I saw a television news story of some parents actually fighting over a few of the remaining "must buys" of that year. I remember one of those parents, looking teary-eyed at the reporter after she had come away empty-handed from her tug-of-war and asking, "What am I going to tell my daughter on Christmas morning?"

My first thought was, Tell her about Grandma Bettye. Then tell her about the Son of God, born in the smelly straw of a barn because there was no room for him to be born in the inn. Tell her about how His family had to flee for their lives, while other children were paying with theirs. For heaven's sake, I thought, tell her! Tell her about a Savior who came to give up His life, so that we may have eternal life—One who came not necessarily to give us everything we want but to bring us everything we really *need*.

The more I think about it, I believe that is a

good agenda not only for Christmas Day and the day after but also for every day of the rest of our lives.

Prayer

With grateful hearts, we come before you, Lord Christ, wanting to bring the very best we have to offer. Please show us how to do so. Amen.

Notes

Introduction

1. Jon M. Walton, "The Unexpected Hour," a copyrighted sermon preached December 3, 1995, at Westminster Presbyterian Church, Wilmington, Delaware.

2. Barbara Brown Taylor, *Bread of Angels* (Cambridge, Mass.: Cowley Publications, 1997), 157.

Day One

3. Fred B. Craddock et al., *Preaching through the Christian Year—A* (Valley Forge, Pa.: Trinity Press International, 1992), 10.

4. Jon M. Walton, an unpublished paper presented to the January 1998 meeting of the Moveable Feast (an annual ministers' study group) in Memphis, Tennessee.

Day Two

5. Dietrich Bonhoeffer, *Letters and Papers from Prison,* ed. Eberhard Bethge (New York: Macmillan, 1953), 72.

6. Albert Curry Winn, *A Christian Primer* (Louisville, Ky.: Westminster/John Knox Press, 1990), 150.

7. Quoted by Ted Wardlaw in an unpublished paper presented to the January 1995 meeting of the Moveable Feast in Holmes, New York.

Day Three

8. Desmond Tutu, "Grace upon Grace," *Journal for Preachers* 15, no. 1 (Advent 1991): 22.

9. Robert Fulghum, *It Was on Fire When I Lay Down on It* (New York: Villard Books, 1990), 74–75.

Day Four

10. Walker Percy, *The Second Coming* (New York: Ivy Books, 1980), 307, 328, as cited by J. Clinton McCann Jr., "Preaching on Psalms for Advent," *Journal for Preachers* 16, no. 1 (Advent 1992): 12.

11. Cited by Lee A. Wyatt, "Are We Having Fun Yet?" *Journal for Preachers* 18, no. 1 (Advent 1994): 18.

12. Vaclav Havel, *Disturbing the Peace* (New York: Alfred A. Knopf, 1990), 181–82. For this citation I am grateful to Christine Chakoian and her unpublished paper for the Second Sunday of Advent presented to the January 1997 meeting of the Moveable Feast in Chicago.

Day Five

13. C. S. Lewis, *The Silver Chair* (New York: Collier Books, 1970), 158–59.

Day Six

14. Clyde Edgerton, *In Memory of Junior* (Chapel Hill, N.C.: Algonquin Books, 1992), 47.

Day Seven

15. William Kethe, "All People That on Earth Do Dwell,"

The Presbyterian Hymnal (Louisville, Ky.: Westminster/John Knox Press, 1990), Hymn 220.

16. Karl Barth, as cited in *Weavings* 2, no. 6 (November/December 1992): 26–27.

Day Eight

17. Jon M. Walton, a sermon on this text preached December 6, 1998, at Westminster Presbyterian Church, Wilmington, Delaware.

18. Rick Spalding, an unpublished paper presented to the January 1998 meeting of the Moveable Feast, Memphis, Tennessee.

Day Nine

19. Thomas G. Long, *Shepherds and Bathrobes: Sermons for Advent, Christmas and Epiphany: Cycle B, Gospel Texts* (Lima, Ohio: C.S.S. Publishing Co., 1987), 20. As cited by Ted Wardlaw in a sermon preached at Central Presbyterian Church in Atlanta, 1992.

Day Ten

21. Stephen R. Covey, *The Seven Habits of Highly Effective People* (New York: Fireside Books, 1989), 33. I am grateful for the citation of the work to Chandler Stokes and his unpublished paper presented to the January 1999 meeting of the Moveable Feast in Ann Arbor, Michigan.

22. I am indebted for this insight to Michael Lindvall and his unpublished paper for the Second Sunday of

Advent presented to the January 1999 meeting of the Moveable Feast in Ann Arbor, Michigan.

Day Eleven

23. Walter Brueggemann et al., *Texts for Preaching (Year A)* (Louisville, Ky.: Westminster John Knox Press, 1995), 10.

Day Twelve

24. Jon M. Walton, a sermon preached November 19, 1998, at Westminster Presbyterian Church, Wilmington, Delaware. This meditation owes its substance to that sermon.

25. Ibid.

Day Thirteen

26. Barbara Brown Taylor, "Come, Lord Jesus," *Journal for Preachers* 20, no. 1 (Advent 1996): 3.

Day Fourteen

27. Taylor, *Bread of Angels*, 93–94.

28. Kathleen Norris, *Amazing Grace: A Vocabulary of Faith* (New York: Riverhead Books, 1998), 76.

Day Fifteen

29. Cited by Stokes, unpublished paper. This day's meditation draws substantially from Stokes's work on this text from John's Gospel.

Day Sixteen

30. Ted Wardlaw, an unpublished paper on this text

presented to the January 1996 meeting of the Moveable Feast in Washington, D.C.

31. Ibid.

Day Seventeen

32. Luke Timothy Johnson, comments made to the January 1998 meeting of the Moveable Feast in Memphis, Tennessee.

Day Eighteen

33. Geoffrey Hill, "Christmas Trees," *The Oxford Book of Christian Verse* (Oxford: Oxford University Press, 1981), 299.

34. Bonhoeffer, *Letters and Papers*, 77–78. My italics.

Day Nineteen

35. Geoffrey Hill, "Lachrimae Amantis," *The Oxford Book of Christian Verse* (Oxford: Oxford University Press, 1981), 299–300.

Day Twenty

36. David Bartlett, personal correspondence, April 30, 1999.

Day Twenty-two

37. Barbara Brown Taylor, *Gospel Medicine* (Cambridge, Mass.: Cowley Publications, 1995), 151–52.

38. Norris, *Amazing Grace*, 30–31. Norris's italics.

Day Twenty-three

39. John Irving, *A Prayer for Owen Meany* (New York:

Ballantine Books, 1989), as cited by K. C. Ptomey in a sermon preached December 24, 1995, at Westminster Presbyterian Church, Nashville, Tennessee.

40. Cited by Chris Chakoian in a sermon on this text preached December 20, 1998, at Community Presbyterian Church, Clarendon Hills, Illinois. Chakoian attributes the story to a sermon preached by John Buchanan on December 17, 1989, at the Fourth Presbyterian Church of Chicago.

41. Taylor, *Gospel Medicine*, 156.

42. W. H. Auden, *For the Time Being: A Christmas Oratorio* (London: Faber & Faber, 1945), 79.

43. Thomas G. Long, *Matthew*, Westminster Bible Companion (Louisville, Ky.: Westminster John Knox Press, 1997), 14.

44. Rick Spalding, unpublished paper presented to the January 1995 meeting of the Moveable Feast in Holmes, New York.

Day Twenty-four

45. Dorothy Sayers, *Kings in Judea*, in *The Man Born to Be King* (New York: Harper & Brothers, 1943), 40. I was directed to this passage by Michael Lindvall in his unpublished paper presented to the January 1996 meeting of the Moveable Feast in Washington, D.C.

46. William Barclay, *The Gospel of Luke* (Philadephia: Westminster Press, 1953), 10.

Day Twenty-five

47. Ann Weems, "What Do I Want for Christmas?" in *Kneeling in Bethlehem* (Philadelphia: Westminster Press, 1987), 34.

48. Jon M. Walton, a sermon preached December 22, 1985, at Westminster Presbyterian Church, Wilmington, Delaware. I am grateful for the citation to Chris Chakoian and her sermon, preached December 21, 1997, at Community Presbyterian Church, Clarendon Hills, Illinois.

Day Twenty-six

49. The Brueghel painting is on permanent display at the Musée de Beaux-Arts in Lille, France. My descriptions of the painting draw upon those of William H. Willimon, *On a Wild and Windy Mountain* (Nashville: Abingdon Press, 1984), 15–17.

50. Joanna Adams, a sermon preached November 29, 1992, at Trinity Presbyterian Church, Atlanta.

51. Kathy Galloway, *Getting Personal: Stories and Meditations* (London: SPCK, 1995), 96.

52. John L. Bell, as cited in Galloway, *Getting Personal*, 96.

Christmas Eve

53. Geoffrey Ainger, "Born in the Night, Mary's Child," *The Presbyterian Hymnal* (Louisville, Ky.: Westminster/ John Knox Press, 1990), Hymn 30.

Christmas Day

54. David Wilcox, "Show the Way," ©1993 Irving Music, Inc.

The Day after Christmas

55. Will Campbell, *Brother to a Dragonfly* (New York: Seabury Press, 1977), 5.